FIVE FIFTY-FIVE

Maura Dooley was born in Truro, grew up in Bristol, worked for some years in Yorkshire, and has lived in London for the past 30 years. She is a freelance writer and lectures at Goldsmiths College. Her selection from earlier work, *Sound Barrier: Poems 1982-2002* (Bloodaxe Books, 2002) drew on collections including *Explaining Magnetism* (1991) and *Kissing a Bone* (1996), both Poetry Book Society Recommendations. *Kissing a Bone* and her later collection *Life Under Water*, a Poetry Book Society Recommendation in 2008, were both shortlisted for the T.S. Eliot Prize. Her poem 'Cleaning Jim Dine's Heart' was shortlisted for the Forward Prize for Best Single Poem in 2015, and was included in *The Silvering* (2016), also a Poetry Book Society Recommendation. Her eighth collection, *Five Fifty-Five*, was published by Bloodaxe in 2023.

She received a Cholmondeley Award from the Society of Authors in 2016. Her translation (with Elhum Shakerifar) of Azita Ghahreman's *Negative of a Group Photograph* (Farsi title: نگاتیوی کی عکس دسته جمعی) was published by Bloodaxe Books with the Poetry Translation Centre in 2018. *Negative of a Group Photograph* received an English PEN Award, and was shortlisted for the Warwick Prize for Women in Translation 2019. She also edited *Making for Planet Alice: New Women Poets* (1997) and *The Honey Gatherers: A Book of Love Poems* (2002) for Bloodaxe, and *How Novelists Work* (2000) for Seren.

MAURA DOOLEY

Five Fifty-Five

BLOODAXE BOOKS

ISBN: 978 1 78037 657 8

First published 2023 by
Bloodaxe Books Ltd,
Eastburn,
South Park,
Hexham,
Northumberland NE46 1BS.

www.bloodaxebooks.com
For further information about Bloodaxe titles
please visit our website and join our mailing list
or write to the above address for a catalogue.

Supported using public funding by
**ARTS COUNCIL
ENGLAND**

Cover design: Neil Astley & Pamela Robertson-Pearce

Printed in Great Britain by Bell & Bain Limited, Glasgow, Scotland, on
acid-free paper sourced from mills with FSC chain of custody certification.

CONTENTS

For David, Imelda and Isadora

Vertaling

I struggle to balance your words on a silver tray.
They tinkle. I fear for a smash and splinters.

Shuffling along trying to match the spring in your step
all the time looking up, keeping my head in the air,

I have filled each one with a drop of something.
A pinch more? Does the flavour seem right?

The scent? Mixing them to a different shade
none is quite as you would have made them.

Shyly, I raise my tray to you. An offering on tin,
buckling a little beneath the weight.

UnEnglished

On the desk a bible in Welsh is open at the Psalms
and like the woman who arrived with a pheasant
and sat to pluck it on the summer lawn – the feathers
taken by the wind to the four corners of the earth
as the naked bird stiffened on the grass –
so I knock at the door of this language, its double dds
and double lls, its simmering beauty, and hear how
to baste and roast it to plump goodness,
the house herby and steamy with new flavours,
sharing the succulent dish with any who would try.

Her Wish for Big Windows

is a denial of swaddling, coddling winter warmth
of hearth and home and the drawing of curtains
in small pretty rooms with their interesting beams

she wants an expanse of rippling glass to show up
cobwebs, bleed the carpet, stripe and strip the spines of books,
hers is the need for a spill, swash, swill of light

never mind the long shady season that is to come,
the shortness of days that no clock can turn back,
each casement, every sash will open wide in that house
the brilliant air will bathe and soothe her smiling, waiting face.

Gaudy Welsh

When you see it, you know the truth of it,
it is the everyday cast as our tomorrows,
as if the sturdy sweetness of a jug of cream
had burst into song,
rose of the dawn sky, blue of the starless,
                        cloud and diamond,
lustre caught in a rim of gold, it is Home
pitched out into the world in its best dress.

It is everyday and it is tomorrow
and when you see it, you know its truth.

The Blue Willow and the Indian Tree

It's all there in the inflorescence,
the ancient tree of life, the lovers
who try to run from family ties,
the fast-flowing water, the bridge.

Our families crossed continents
in tableware, their Delft, their China,
a story, their story a mystery and overhead always
the birds, wheeling, calling, waiting to land.

Uncle Tom Writes Home

Bakersfield, California, 17 July 1919

You will think I am a long time answering your letter.

Yes, I am still living and in good health now but had been given up by the doctor, having had the Influenza.

We all had it, it was an epidemic.

I am awful lonesome now.

I suppose as you grow older you get lonesome. If you have not made a fortune or money enough to fight the future.

I look back. In this long life it took every cent just to make ends meet and get along.

And oh that War, how it made things so terrible hard.

You say all the old neighbours are dead and gone?

God Rest them.

I see the Conways are well, same old friends as long ago.

God Bless them.

You ask about Uncle Ned. I never saw him. Everyone lost track of Ned, even Alice.

Alice is dead and Aunt Mary and all the family is dead. Only Tom.

I see all the Powers girls are gone but one. I will soon have to go myself. I don't know but hope we will have a happier place in the life to come.

Is the *Hen and Chickens* on the Carrick Road still there? A girl by the name of Mary was proprietress when I was home. Pierce Powers wanted me to make a match with her.

He is dead I suppose?

I feel awful bad for many things but most particularly that I am not in a financial circumstance to be able to send you some money. I hope the boys will be able to keep you in happiness.

I am always thinking of the dear people I used to know. What a different world now.

Your loving brother

Fam

Light on the horizon
as you stand on the shore.

It doesn't need hunger
to scatter a nation

but the insidious drip
of rain, rot, misfortune,

not the palm held out
just the fist.

Quiver

An Irishman in the British Army
in exchange for boots and warmth.
Or, an Irish boy maybe, five foot five,
lying about his age, hungry. An Irish boy.
Ypres, Somme, Abancourt.

An Irishman in the British Army
'of good character', is disciplined for drink
when his father dies in the workhouse,
'of good character', is confined to barracks
when Casement is hanged.

An Irishman in the British Army,
is released and in the steamy soup kitchen
– the room quivers – when a girl lifts
her head to look back at him.
Swimmily. She'll do fine. He pictures her,

steady at a stove somewhere,
they'll plant a row of scallions, lilies maybe,
watch the waves from a shore he can't name,
through steam he pictures her steady,
somewhere. A quiver.

An Irishman in the British Army
never to be welcomed home, sees Ireland
just once more, swimmily, could not picture
me, a little way down the line somewhere,
looking back at him, steadily, released.

Abecedarium

Once you learn to read you will be forever free

attr. FREDERICK DOUGLASS

X marks the spot where treasure might be found
where words from weeds begin to stir
and books open their leaves to the sun.
X magnifies the field of vision tenfold.

X-Irishman is what an uncle gained
in 'signing up': three meals a day, a roof,
another nation – but made his mark
by handing on where treasure might be found
in schools and libraries and polling station.

X magnifies the field of vision tenfold,
we see the horizontal axis, skull & crossbones,
poison, fast cars, adult danger,
X magnifies the field of vision tenfold,
the pharmacy, the occult, babe in a manger,
another kind of wrong, a sign of love,
and X the algebraic unknown,

while here's my chromosomes and
(fingers crossed behind my back)
a photo of my heart you can't yet read
– nor what's written in the asterisks above –

though in cursive, capitals, in abcdery,
it's all unravelled now, fiction or fact,
X marked the spot where treasure could be found
we can decipher molten words, we're free to act.

∞

an idea that is myth that is an idea
that turns back on itself and out again
and is a vision, a story, crest of a wave,
the salt ripple, or the wave itself, the slap-splash
to the face, tug of the moon, turn of the tide,
the moment's sparkle, aphelion, perihelion, aphelion,
herring in shoal and the herring gull diving
floating, soaring, the west wind at ease
or the fresh draught from the east that turns back
on itself, is Amergin, an idea that is myth
that is words in air, in the margin of a psalter,
illumination, mist clearing over valley and field,
over factory and airstrip, is the wren's egg in the nest
of a rowan tree, the tap-tap of release and a single feather
surfing a mountain stream to the travellers' camp,
the city street, the emigrant/immigrant ship,
the laptop's glow, to an idea that is a myth that is

Casey, Cullen & the Eighth

Cullen and daughter are back for repeal of the Eighth,
daughter anyway. It's an excuse for visiting Casey
and a round of golf, Cullen anyway.
For Casey, golf is another amendment altogether,
but there's the bar. The bar's where the talking gets done,

who's left of the old crowd and does he remember?
Some questions are never chanced between them till Cullen asks,
'Do you ever hear of Anne Salmon?' Casey shakes his head
hadn't thought of Anne in years but suddenly something

comes clear to him, the journey, a slip upstream
and away, darting through the clear pools, sliding
under rocks and boulders, clearing weed, waiting, waiting
for that stretch of sweet open water. Never looking back.

Tending the Border

The door to the walled garden is open today.
Cleanly, you've dug out the Creeping Jenny,
Cleavers, Bitter Cress, anything carelessly walked in.

Verbena bonariensis, Asteraceae, Phlox paniculata,
are bedded down, their fragrant, complicated language
a new fence, artful in its buttoned-up undoneness.

Restoration

In the garden at Strokestown Park
where the slow recreation of lost days grows
with the turn of each season,

John slips an Irish apple tree between
the rows of Heritage Correct Old English.
Bud little tree. Feed the land.

A Ruined Castle in Wales

and another dank cellar whose purpose
is uncertain, where clouds cloak the walls
in rain and farmers lift fallen stone
for their own repairs, where rooks pick over
scattered twigs, centuries jumble in
the dressing-up box and at the gift shop
there are dragons, blankets, ice cream.

Those times will come again.
When will those times come again?
These times will never come again.

Some Things Learnt at Lumb Bank

Our land was churned and muddied by an old nag
and Stephen taught me a new word, *horsification*.

Jim sucked out the septic tank to spray his fields,
whereon potatoes thrived and were delicious.

Weekly, John walked five miles from Todmorden
to feed his heifers: died in his chair, clogs on.

The eggs that hatched as baby roosters crowed angrily,
good for only fox or pot.

The leaves that soothed a nettle rash were better buttered,
served as pudding.

Our days were bright and green as the hills on which (remember?)
snow once fell for eight weeks straight. Our faces glowed.

The Rosebud at Jane Austen's House

> There was a motif they could not make sense of. It was a
> manufacturing fault in the paper
>
> MARY GUYATT,
> Curator, Jane Austen House Museum

Back through the velvet embossed, the anaglypta,
the lincrusta or down further, through a field of flowers
to the dust and mould of soft distemper on early plaster.
You may have tackled it yourself with a hired steamer?

Did every layer hold its story tight or did the voices whisper?
The maid who swiped at soot and wiped off mud,
a yeoman loosening boots to sleep by the hearth,
the family gathering close to share a candle?

Here, on scraps of paper, scholarship reveals the need
to trim a budget with work of an apprentice, whose
repeat, repeat, repeat, repeat of trellis is intricate
but empty, for at its heart is the absent rose.

At the Minster Gate Bookshop

The spring crocus were slim spines of green and orange,
our blue skies Hoggart, Hobsbaum, Laing, Ford,
autumn came with the sound of turning leaves
winter brought a crowd to warm their hands
and sometimes steal. The Emily Dickinson thief had made
herself a coat of felt in which to slip the Roberts
edition, *Ivory boards. Top edge gilt. Near fine.* Vivaldi
and Bach soothed the frayed nerves of King Penguin
hunters, Signed First collectors, Saturday browsers
or students rummaging for Baldwin and Spark. Rackhams
and Leightons, rested their *only slightly rubbed* shoulders.
Everywhere Garamond outfoxed us all in buckram,
Morocco, velvet or vellum and yet could barely hold
that flock of words – wild words! – that roar of words.

L'Heure Bleue

Never let anyone tell you that North Cornwall is warm –
it is not'

JEAN RHYS
Letter to Selma Vaz Dias, 16 October 1956

Not Paris, here the hour between dog and wolf
is bitter blue, a wind that silks about the neck
and tightens
            and years pass in that indeterminate light
in which she comes to see
                 that Bertha too was cold,
fire 'the only warmth she knows in England'.

She lights a small flame then
                  that even the wind coming
'straight across the Atlantic at ninety miles an hour'
cannot extinguish and watches it catch fire.

Redhead by the Side of the Road

Tired of Lockdown
               when Anne swings by
to run with me a daily loop
of suburban streets
               of small hurts and pleasures,
of larger hidden griefs,

under the railway arch, down a back lane,
past the trembling candles of horse chestnut trees,
                     dear old friend,
who makes me smile to see
that only when we get up close
          will the everyday, the ordinary, shine.

Ghost Writer

Reading you, I could not read at all.
Novels fell from my hands, my eyes
snagged on any sentence
                              and music?
Music was a tune I could not catch
nor fix a note to (your trials, your joys,
your fears, all mine),
                              my voice then
a foreign thing and not my own.

So now you're gone, I take down
this big book, the one you left, the empty one,
I take down this big book and write in it.

At Orchard House

– if you are a skilful gleaner, you may get many a pocket-full even of grafted fruit, long after apples are supposed to be gone out-of-doors.

HENRY THOREAU, *Wild Apples*

A mother, a fever,
the tattoo of feet on stairs,
a swing round the banisters
and down to a fire in the parlour
or out to the apple orchard
the plait of voices, laughter,
anger, always forgiveness in
a mother's voice, reading

reading of one whose shoes
you stood in to be bold
or sensible or dreamy, for isn't it

just as you'd imagined,
buttoned boots in a sisterly row,
Marmee's spice chest
out on the table, Baldwin trees
bright with blossom, the trill and tang
of remembered voices each a braid
in your own mother's voice,
every room a new chapter?

Or not at all as you'd imagined,
desk, hearth, shelf of books,
planting of seeds, swell of ideas?
Yet through an open door
how well you seem to know it

all that was sharp, then rosy,
then ready for the taking
was there all the time
in a mother's voice reading.

That orchard turned from green to gold.
Louisa picked fruit carefully
to settle the doctor's bill,
easy to harvest all that surrounds you,
harder to send it ripe and delicious down the years.

Mayday in Ravenna

and if I were to call to mind that town, Jo,
I'd see us walk again down streets of flowers
looking for Dante, one springtime, years ago,

Sisson in hand and darting through the showers.
Foolish tourists, who nevertheless understood
to make of this journey something that was ours

that words might light a candle in a dark wood
and friendship be a witness to the hours
spent seeking Virgil on our winding road.

Roses lined the cafés, music filled the bars,
the long day ending, all our talking done,
under lowering cloud, eyes tilted to the stars,

Dante slept, rain fell, as we strolled slowly on.

Come Fill the Cup

... so when he asked, 'what would you like?'
I answered, 'different view?'
and he's, 'sure, table by the window?' and
smiling, 'what do you want with it?'
I should have said ... wanted to say,
Thou beside me singing in the wilderness
but looking away through the glass,
I heard my voice speak quietly,
 'A jug of wine? Some bread?'
so here I am. Same view.

Unacknowledged Legislators

I'm in a rented car in backlane San Climente,
pre-election glum, when Paul Muldoon's voice
enters the dusty Seat, speaking slowly for
a Spanish translator who somersaults sentences
in and out of the aircon.
              A bend in the road
and sunlight tunes the empty cove before us
to opalescence.
              The radio's voice shimmers
as it tells us how he's never really understood
why poets should be asked to save the world:

We don't ask the painters, we don't ask the composers,
we don't even ask the pop stars. Give us a break!

Mythology

I'd like to know whether Paul climbed back in through the
window Louis gazed out from, or whether, in fact, that snow
fell in Birmingham not Belfast.

I think those dolphins you watched for, and movingly failed to
see, annoyingly followed the boat after all, David, didn't they?

Edward's train that unwontedly paused to allow him reflection
one meadowsweet day in high June, was timetabled to do so

and though plums sit in the mind so sweet and so cold, maybe
those were grapes, actually,

that she left in the icebox?

There is more than glass between the snow and the huge roses.

Thirty-six Views of Mount Fuji

On a beaten-up lacquered box in the bottom of a drawer

In Lafcadio Hearn from Penguin Classics

On place mats at the noodle bar

In TripAdvisor on iPhone

On chopsticks from Tokyo airport

In the *Essential Haiku* of Robert Hass

*

Here are the matters
of the world, the mind looks at
the mystery of this world.

*

Behind a folding screen

Beneath the drying persimmon

Inside an unfurling fan

Above the autumn rain cloud

Under a wan winter sun

Within the scent of plum blossom

*

Looking at this life
as light moves on a mountain,
cut flowers, snowfall.

*

The crane and the koi

The red shadow of the maple

The pine tree, the stork

The bamboo and the sparrow

Swirling petals, falling leaves

Hidden, hidden, hidden

*

Basho writes, *misty,*
I cannot see Fuji-san.
How interesting.

*

Hokusai, unwell, alone, watches the mountain

Rainstorm beneath the Summit

Ricefields

Cushion Pine

Morning after a Snowstorm

Red Fuji

*

Famously, in Prussian
Blue, sea spray becomes snow,
Fuji is Japan.

*

Without cherry blossom, it was the wrong season

Kusama's seven love letters were unknown to me then

By day the mountain slept on sunlit pillows

By night the stars were screened by rain

As I crossed *the Bridge of Dreams* I saw

Thirty-six views of Mount Fuji

The moon was tethered,
a boat in nightsky held in
check, chill winds rising.

*

Screens roll back, a fan
unfolds, the mountain sees plain
the matter of this world.

A Year in Mr Inoue's Haiku

Snowflakes fall in Spring
bright and light as eider down
they fill the valley.

Seeds planted softly
help the deepest roots hold firm
when that keen wind blows.

O, rosemary branch!
How you bring to mind a lost
sweet voice, remembrance.

Wisteria blooms,
the mosquito's whirring song
hangs in scented air.

Swishswash, raindrops spill
into the brimming river
to become as one.

Under shadowy
darkness of mountains and trees
winter is deepening.

Fine Wind, Clear Morning

On such a morning
clear as a glass of fresh water
I see my mother in her garden,
so many years away, bend to take
a sprig of mint.

                At her touch,
between thumb and finger
the scent whorls, spirals
turns on a westward breeze
to reach me here.

Perennial, restorative, familiar,
my mother hands to me a sprig of mint.

Song in an Old Tradition

The shirt of my girl
I soak and I scrub
I pound and I drub
I rinse and I spin.

The shirt of my girl
I hang out to air
and still I breathe in
the scent of her there.

Span

She has sent a postcard from Venice,
narrow alleys, walls peeling,
a picturesque decay,

Ponte something leaping a canal
and although I think I know that bridge
(I've crossed it)

it could be one of hundreds stretching
over oily water in sunlight, under
the sad flap of damp washing

and that familiar gasp, that little arching
ache, was learnt aged six, when the car
met a hump-back and made that moment

suddenly all that was needed:
heart in the present, hope in the future,
a miracle of engineering.

Counting Down

Every human has a finite number of heartbeats

BUZZ ALDRIN

1 *Bildungsroman*

America was stranger, more mysterious
than that old familiar face.
                              Nights following
we looked up at her peaches and cream
                                        blueing,
her pits and blemishes,
                    knowing she'd been trampled on
left bruised
        but still we chorused
                            'lift off!'
in borrowed voices
while the tide continued in and out,
                          rising and falling,
and our own inner seas began to form.

2 *Reifungsroman*

No one I knew then had died.
I think of the deep space known to me now
                        as darkness,
how neither   *infinite*   nor   *fathomless*
no word   quite suggests that stillness
broken only now and then
                        by a shrug from the gods,
            a meteor shower,
Perseids which freckle a warm July sky,
        pierce the indigo border between us,
    particles of light that fall on me
even as I look up into the unknown.

43

Blink

We are only here a minute.
In a daughter strolled,
her sister   a beat later,
while out into the dusk
my Daddy walked and then
more cautiously, my mother.

A bike, a car, two houses,
all outgrown and friends
whose patience snapped
though some hung on,
through *sturm und drang*.

The stock exchange went up
and down, statues were smashed
and new ones forged,
crowds starved, crowds fled
and some were even saved by hope,
hope and its torn sail out on a wild sea

look, there, as night draws in,
the ocean's still, starlings massing
their liquid flight darkening to a bruise.

Hard Shoulder

A strip of hesitation
as much as vegetation,
though no one paused long
to dump this rug or move
that fox out of the fast lane,
curled now, like a blood moon,
fallen amongst loosestrife and grit.
Verge, whether frame or margin,
its brilliant green pathways
stretch to vanishing point
and here we are, on it.

The Forests of South London

Shaggy acorn cups of Turkey oak mulch
the roots of chestnut, alder, willow, ash,
a fancy strain brought in for hardiness.
Over centuries they arrive, the introduced,
the invited, *continental* or *exotic*, useful maybe,
or like a breath of fresh air, *bohemian*,
and others, mere blow-ins, taking root,
scattering seed *right, left and centre.*
There have been more formal arrangements,
coppiced, pollarded, espaliered even, yet now
slim shoots, electric with their own beauty,
bend in the newest breeze and blossom.
See how our colours fill the summer streets,
the sweet strength of us massing and blooming.

A-Sighing-and-a-Sobbing

Gather old friends   linnet, sparrow, thrush,
      all vanished others
            whose flicker or flash
once lit field and bush.

We didn't notice
      your muted greeting at dawn,
            your absence at harvest,
      only the empty lawn.

Gather wing, gather beak, gather egg,
      find us again in our bankruptcy,
feather our nest.

Autumn in the Absent Elms

After-comers cannot guess the beauty been

GERARD MANLEY HOPKINS,
'Binsey Poplars'

Their soft green bells toll unheard

mist   moist   frost   last   lost

Seasonal

You've taken up residence in that wood stack.
                    The darkest corner
where woodlice run circles round you
                    and under the ochre
drip of winter rain you let a rat piss,
a cat sharpen his claws,
a spider spin a web with you at its centre.
                    Heart of Oak

Green Man
            you've taken root in shadowland,
feel sap rise in your veins like a lost language,
shake out your frothy new leaves for spring.

The Unforgotten

'Take courage'

ANNE BRONTË
– her last words to her sister Charlotte

At Anne Brontë's grave, in the salt air she loved,
where the words were almost lost from the stone,
dissolving, you first kissed me
            and once, we took my parents to see
the rain, the moorland, the tiny writing we struggled to read,
stepping out dazed into that garden of tombs
gleaming, in the damp light
            and sometimes, I swipe at crumbs or dry plates
with my souvenir linen image of three melded heads,
fading, indistinct,
            but today, I open a beaten copy
of *The Novels of the Brontë Sisters* (Pilot 1947),
the only thing left of my Grandmother's time on earth,
to read, in her bold emphatic hand,
'Nearer than the living are the unforgotten dead.
Their presence is ever with you
and they walk always at your side.'

By Way of Kensal Green

(i.m. Sarah Maguire)

a bitter day
                    when the rag tag of us
spill out to a reel of rose gold cloud
moon on the rise through the blue hour
parakeets leafing empty branches
                    kaleidoscopic chatter
all the colours, all the songs,
and you'd have liked your old friend's joke
that now this motley crew would have to go home
                    and write poems about the jewelled evening
the sharp air, the busy music of the trees, the afterwards

In the Blue Vase

Where a graceful head rests
on the rim, the vase reflects
the garden, draws the outside in
from where each seed you've sown
or scattered, windblown, finds a foot in
earth, is finding its own place in earth.
The sun moves, the bees dance,
the delicate stems strengthen,
even in all this rain (the tea cooling),
the tender roots take hold.
The blue vase will be filled with all
your flowers, Helen, blooming.

Did You Know Ann Atkinson?

In a bar in Singapore
which certainly involved the cliché
of a Gin Sling and a stranger introducing themselves
and one thing leading to another,
it was to a face from twenty-five years before
and a poem, more than one, and later a book
and a memory (specific) and the poem
itself a message in a bottle, a ship in a bottle,
sails furled for the passage
into that small space,
unfolding then like a fresh page,
like a fallen leaf, green again, in the steam rising
from the newly-rinsed streets of a rainy season.

A Haunted House

Not that I didn't know it was there,
the other side of the veil,
mist   mizzle
the start of migraine

not that I didn't know it,
dream   cloud
a change in the weather

not that I didn't remember
pressed between pages
sepal   petal

not that I didn't   that it might
fade   slip
gathered, scattered, squandered

not that I   not that   not
not that I didn't worry
that it was extinguished
the light in the heart

I've Been Thinking a Lot About Heaven

I watched him tidy up his sorrow,
tuck it into his pocket, slide it into a pit
cleared for the bulb of a snowdrop
but grief is slippery, ungainly, ugly.
O chokey, noisy, bullying grief!

I'm thinking a lot about Heaven
while this train cuts a line from
Doncaster to Retford, through a blur
of mist on the meadows and towns.
Last night's rain and morning dew

and the suddenness of swifts is a curlicue
on blue, blue which I know
is a matter of wavelength and molecule
but which is also distance, *blue-remembered*,
and an unknown spire piercing the heart.

Five Fifty-Five

Last of the sun, flintlight on a bright field
before evening   before   but not yet, not yet.

Here where houses spill kitchenlight
                   across a cloud of leaves,
                          gusting
into the violet hour   not yet, not yet
        the vespery flight
        of sloughed off skins,
for even as oak and alder hold tight to ochre and amber
        in not-yet-winter
             leaves are skipping a fairytale path to my door,
                a door that opens to let a slice of warmth
           hold back the falling darkness
hold back from
             not yet, not-yet-winter
and though summer may be over
            still the roses keep insisting, insisting.

A Bunch of Consolation

You think they'll always be there,
(the ones who always have been).
They showed you the way,
not their way
but how to find your own
(and what to say),
sweeping the path of leaves
                      or snow
but then they leave, they go,
before you were ready
(how could you ever be ready?)
to wonder, wondering,
what have you learned exactly?
To love, to speak up, to hold steady.
                Hold steady.

NOTES

Vertaling (9) is the Dutch word for a translation or version.

Gaudy Welsh (12) is the overall name given to mid-19th-century Welsh household china, hand painted in cobalt blue, copper lustre, yellow, burnt orange and green.

Uncle Tom Writes Home (15) is taken entirely from a letter sent home from California to my Great Grandfather in Ireland.

Casey, Cullen & the Eighth (20): 'The Repeal of the Eighth' refers to the 1983 constitutional amendment which guaranteed the right to life of the unborn, making abortion illegal unless the pregnancy was life-threatening. In 2018 a referendum was held, after which, the Thirty-sixth amendment of the Constitution of Ireland was passed which repealed the Eighth amendment. Many Irish people, working away, returned home to take part in the vote. Casey, Cullen, Ward and McKeogh are four imaginary friends whose lives I drop in on periodically to see what they're up to.

Some Things Learnt at Lumb Bank (24) is for David Hunter, David and Tina Pease, Carol Hughes, Liz Almond and Shirley Fawthrop, about a time at Lumb Bank, Ted Hughes's former home, run as a writing centre by the Arvon Foundation.

L'Heure Bleue (27) is the twilight hour as well as the name of a scent by Guerlain loved by Jean Rhys. Quotations in the poem are from letters to her daughter Maryvonne Moerman (16 October 1956) and to Selma Vaz Dias (9 April 1958). Bertha Mason, the first Mrs Rochester in *Jane Eyre*, is reinvented by Jean Rhys as Antoinette Cosway, in *Wide Sargasso Sea*.

Redhead by the Side of the Road (28) is the title of a novel by Anne Tyler, the reading of which was a comfort during Lockdown 2020.

At Orchard House (31): Louisa May Alcott wrote *Little Women* (1868) at Orchard House, Concord, Massachusetts, and lived there with her family from 1858 to 1877, supporting them through her writing.

Come Fill the Cup (33) is a line from the *Rubáiyát* of Omar Kháyyám translated by Edward Fitzgerald, as are other quotations italicised within the poem.

Mythology (35) closes with a line from Louis MacNeices's poem 'Snow'.

Thirty-six Views of Mount Fuji (36) was written in response to a series of landscape prints by the Japanese artist Hokusai. His *Thirty-six Views of Mount Fuji* shows Mount Fuji seen from different locations and in different seasons and weathers. The colour Prussian Blue had recently been introduced to Japan and Hokusai explored its use in the prints which added to their immediate popularity. 'The Floating Bridge of Dreams' is the title of the final chapter of *The Tale of Genji* written by a lady of the Japanese court around 1000 AD, an image of the transience of human life.

A Year in Mr Inoue's Haiku (39): Yasuaki Inoue has published two collections of poetry, *Shiho* and *Kyoguko*. He is a Haiku Master and President of the Haiku society, Kakko. Professor Michiyo Takano of Yamanashi Prefecture University provided literal translations and much helpful discussion.

Fine Wind, Clear Morning (40) takes its title from a Hokusai print also known as Red Fuji.

Counting Down (43): The critic Barbara Frey Waxman coined 'Reifungsroman' to suggest the concept of a story of ripening as women grow older.

In the Blue Vase (52) was written in response to Helen Dunmore's poem 'My Life's Stem Was Cut'.

Did You Know Ann Atkinson? (53): Ann Atkinson was a poet and musician, Poet Laureate of both the Peak District and of Derbyshire. Her work is published by The Poetry Business.

A Haunted House (54) is the title of a short story by Virginia Woolf, the words in italics are taken from that story and another, 'Monday or Tuesday'.

A Bunch of Consolation (57) takes its title from a line in Adrian Mitchell's poem 'Beattie is Three'.

ACKNOWLEDGEMENTS

'Abecedarium' was commissioned by the Manchester Ripples of Hope Festival (2021) as a response to article 26 of the Universal Declaration of Human Rights. 'A Haunted House' is the title of a short story by Virginia Woolf, one of a number of texts responded to by artists of the New Modernist Network. This poem, invited by Professor Bryony Randall, took off from the work of Anna Chapman Parker and Becky Brewis and was included in the exhibition, *Imprints: Art editing Modernism* (University of Glasgow/ Laurence Sterne Trust/Shandy Hall, 2021).

Many thanks to the editors of the following publications where versions of some of these poems first appeared: *Armistice: A Laureate's Choice of Poems of War and Peace* (Faber, 2018), *Divining Dante* (Recent Work Press, 2021), *Giant Steps: Fifty poets reflect on the Apollo 11 moon landing and beyond* (Recent Work Press, 2019), *The Idler, Lives of Houses* (Princeton University Press, 2020), *Magma, The North, Off the Shelf: A Celebration of Bookshops in Verse* (Picador, 2016), *Poetry Birmingham Literary Journal, Poetry Ireland Review, The Poetry Review, The Rialto, Sleeping in Frozen Quiet* (Wordspace/Indigo Dreams, 2022), *Temenos, The Tree Line: Poems for Trees, Woods & People* (Worple Press, 2017) and *The Washington Post*.

'Mayday in Ravenna' was written for Jo Shapcott, 'At the Minster Gate Bookshop' for Nigel Wallace, 'Gaudy Welsh' for Gillian Clarke and '∞' for Paddy Bushe and Fiona de Buis.

Heartfelt thanks to my beloved family and friends, to my poet brothers Terence and Tim, to Professors Hermione Lee and Helen Carr and to my dear colleagues and students at Goldsmiths, University of London, from whom I have learnt so much.

Thank you, Neil Astley. Bloodaxe is a marvel.